- insights into feelings and motives of characters
- understanding of a wider range of stories

Rereading and rehearing helps children develop automatic word recognition and gives them models of fluent, expressive reading.

Comprehension strategies

Story	Comprehension strategies taught through these Group/Guided Reading Notes				
	Prediction	Questioning	Clarifying	Summarising	Imagining
Green Island	✓	✓	✓	✓	
Storm Castle	✓	✓	✓	✓	✓
Superdog	✓	✓	✓	✓	
The Litter Queen	✓	✓	✓	✓	
The Quest	✓	✓	✓	✓	
Survival Adventure	✓	✓	✓	✓	✓

Vocabulary and phonic opportunities

Each story contains many decodable words, providing lots of opportunities to practice phonic and word recognition skills. The chart shows the tricky words used in each book. The tricky words are common but do not conform to the phonic rules taught up to this point – children will need support to learn and recognise them. If children struggle with one of these words you can model how to read it.

Green Island	Tricky words	adventure, because, caught, climbed, could, dangerous, excited, famous, feathers, guitar, hungry, island, knew, large, money, newspaper, night, oars, oil, party, police, school, secret, squares, stories, tired, treasure, walk, wildlife, worked
Storm Castle	Tricky words	danger, enormous, favourite, frightening, giant, keyhole, laughed, mirror, nasty-looking, robot, school, square
Superdog	Tricky words	believe, buildings, cheering, city, course, fence, giant, girder, hero, minute, newspaper, offering, peace, pictures, quiet, rescue, rolled, service, television, yawned
The Litter Queen	Tricky words	because, centre, climbed, competition, countryside, dangerous, fields, frightened, love, meadows, microlight, nightmare, sandwiches, special, spreading, temperature, throughout, tight, wrappers
The Quest	Tricky words	beautiful, believe, castle, charged, crystal, frightened, galloped, gasped, gnome, journey, knight, meant, mirror, rescue, saucers, secret, swamp, unicorn
Survival Adventure	Tricky words	blueberries, cruel, friendly, frightened, honey, journey, mirror, quiet, survival, wander, wonder, worried

Stage 9

Stories

Gill Howell

Group/Guided Reading Notes

Contents

Introduction	2
Comprehension strategies	3
Vocabulary and phonic opportunities	4
Curriculum coverage chart	5

Green Island
Group or guided reading	8
Group and independent reading activities	9
Speaking, listening and drama activities	11
Writing activities	11

Storm Castle
Group or guided reading	12
Group and independent reading activities	13
Speaking, listening and drama activities	15
Writing activities	15

Superdog
Group or guided reading	16
Group and independent reading activities	17
Speaking, listening and drama activities	19
Writing activities	19

The Litter Queen
Group or guided reading	20
Group and independent reading activities	21
Speaking, listening and drama activities	22
Writing activities	23

The Quest
Group or guided reading	24
Group and independent reading activities	25
Speaking, listening and drama activities	27
Writing activities	27

Survival Adventure
Group or guided reading	28
Group and independent reading activities	29
Speaking, listening and drama activities	30
Writing activities	31

Introduction

Oxford Reading Tree stories at Stages 5 to 9 continue to feature the familiar characters from previous stages in stories that reflect the experiences of most children. The magic key, discovered at Stage 4, also takes children into exciting fantasy adventures, widening and enriching their reading experience.

The stories still use natural language, phonically decodable words and high frequency words, all illustrated with funny and engaging pictures. Reading them will enable children to practise different reading skills, and continue to develop their word recognition and language comprehension.

Using the books

This booklet provides suggestions for using the books for guided, group and independent activities. The reading activities include ideas for developing children's *word recognition* **W** and *language comprehension* **C** skills. Within word recognition, there are ideas for helping children practise their phonic skills and knowledge, as well as helping them to tackle words that are not easy to decode phonically. The language comprehension ideas include suggestions for teaching the skills of prediction, questioning, clarifying, summarising and imagining in order to help children understand the text and the whole stories. Suggestions are also provided for speaking, listening, drama and writing activities.

Reading fluency

To support children in developing fluency in their reading, give them plenty of opportunities to revisit the stories. This includes:
- Rereading independently
- awareness of more complex sentences
- awareness of more complex plots
- awareness of other viewpoints

Curriculum coverage chart

	Speaking, listening, drama	Reading	Writing
Green Island			
PNS Literacy Framework (Y2)	4.1	ⓦ 5.3, 5.4, 5.5 ⓒ 7.1, 7.2, 7.4, 7.5	9.1, 11.1
National Curriculum	Working within level 2		
Scotland (5–14)	Level A/B	Level A/B	Level A/B
N. Ireland (P3/Y3)	1, 2, 3, 5, 6, 7, 10, 11	1, 2, 3, 4, 5, 8, 10, 12, 14, 15, 16, 17	1, 2, 5, 6, 7, 10, 11, 13
Wales (Key Stage 1)	Range: 1, 5 Skills: 2, 5	Range: 1, 2, 6 Skills: 1, 2	Range: 1, 2, 3, 6 Skills: 1, 7, 8
Storm Castle			
PNS Literacy Framework (Y2)	1.3, 2.1, 3.2	ⓦ 5.5, 6.2 ⓒ 7.1, 7.2, 8.2	9.3
National Curriculum	Working towards Level 2		
Scotland (5–14)	Level A/B	Level A/B	Level A/B
N. Ireland (P3/Y3)	1, 2, 5, 6, 10, 11, 12	1, 2, 3, 4, 5, 8, 11, 12, 14, 15, 16, 17	1, 2, 3, 4, 5, 10, 11, 13
Wales (Key Stage 1)	Range: 1, 3 Skills: 2, 3, 5	Range: 1, 2, 6 Skills: 1, 2	Range: 1, 2, 3, 4 Skills: 1, 5, 6

> **Key**
>
> ⓒ = Language comprehension   Y = Year
>
> ⓦ = Word recognition   P = Primary
>
> In the designations such as 5.2, the first number represents the strand and the second number the individual objective

Curriculum coverage chart

	Speaking, listening, drama	Reading	Writing
Superdog			
PNS Literacy Framework (Y2)	1.2	(W) 5.2, 5.4, 5.5 (C) 8.1	9.2, 11.1
National Curriculum	Working towards level 2		
Scotland (5–14)	Level A/B	Level A/B	Level A/B
N. Ireland (P3/Y3)	1, 2, 3, 5, 6, 7, 10, 11	1, 2, 3, 4, 8, 9, 10, 11, 12, 14, 15, 16, 17	1, 3, 5, 6, 7, 8, 10, 11, 12, 13
Wales (Key Stage 1)	Range: 1 Skills: 1, 3	Range: 1, 2, 6 Skills: 1, 2	Range: 1, 2, 3 Skills: 1, 4
The Litter Queen			
PNS Literacy Framework (Y2)	2.1	(W) 6.1 (C) 7.1, 7.4	9.1, 9.2, 9.3, 11.3
National Curriculum	Working towards Level 2		
Scotland (5–14)	Level A/B	Level A/B	Level A/B
N. Ireland (P3/Y3)	1, 2, 5, 6, 10, 11, 12	1, 2, 3, 4, 5, 8, 10, 11, 12, 14, 15, 16, 17	1, 2, 3, 4, 5, 6, 8, 10, 11, 13
Wales (Key Stage 1)	Range: 3 Skills: 2, 3, 5	Range: 1, 2, 6 Skills: 1, 2	Range: 1, 3, 4, 5 Skills: 1, 5, 6

Curriculum coverage chart

	Speaking, listening, drama	Reading	Writing
The Quest			
PNS Literacy Framework (Y2)	4.1	(W) 5.5, 6.1, 6.2 (C) 7.1, 8.3	9.1, 10.1
National Curriculum	Working within level 2		
Scotland (5–14)	Level A/B	Level A/B	Level A/B
N. Ireland (P3/Y3)	1, 2, 3, 5, 6, 7, 10, 11	1, 2, 3, 4, 5, 8, 10, 11, 12, 14, 15, 16, 17	1, 2, 3, 5, 6, 7, 8, 10, 11, 12, 13
Wales (Key Stage 1)	Range: 1, 5 Skills: 2, 6	Range: 1, 2, 4, 6 Skills: 1, 2	Range: 1, 2, 3 Skills: 1, 5
Survival Adventure			
PNS Literacy Framework (Y2)	1.3, 2.1, 3,1	(W) 5.5, 6.1 (C) 7.5, 8.2	9.1, 10.1
National Curriculum	Working towards Level 2		
Scotland (5–14)	Level A/B	Level A/B	Level A/B
N. Ireland (P3/Y3)	1, 2, 3, 5, 6, 8, 9, 10, 11	1, 2, 3, 4, 5, 7, 8, 10, 11, 12, 14, 15, 16, 17	1, 2, 3, 5, 6, 7, 8, 10, 11, 12, 13
Wales (Key Stage 1)	Range: 2, 5 Skills: 1, 2	Range: 1, 2, 4, 6 Skills: 1, 2	Range: 1, 2, 3, 7 Skills: 1, 4

Green Island

> **C** = Language comprehension   *R, AF* = QCA reading assessment focus
>
> **W** = Word recognition   *W, AF* = QCA writing assessment focus

Group or guided reading

Introducing the book

C *(Clarifying)* Together, look at the cover. Talk about who is in the illustration. Ask the children: *Do you think this is a family outing or a school outing?*

C *(Prediction, Clarifying)* Read the title and discuss what the story might be about. Look through the book to see if the children are right.

Strategy check

● Remind children to use different strategies to work out new words.

Independent reading

● Ask children to read the story aloud. Praise and encourage them while they read, and prompt as necessary.

● If the children have difficulty with a word, encourage them to think of ways to work out what the word means, such as split it up into syllables.

C *(Summarising)* Ask children to retell the story in no more than 10 sentences.

Assessment Check that children:

● *(R, AF1)* use a range of strategies to read for meaning

● *(R, AF3)* use comprehension skills to work out what is happening in the story.

Returning to the text

C *(Questioning, Clarifying)* Ask: *How did the children feel about the school outing at the start of the story? How do you know? How did Mrs Honey help wildlife? Show me the part of the story that tells us.*

W Find 'feathers' on page 10. Ask a volunteer to suggest a strategy for working it out and to read the word.

W Find the word 'treasure' on page 18 and ask another child to read it. Ask: *How is it similar to and different from the word 'feathers'?* Ask: *What other words end with 'sure'?* (e.g. measure, leisure).

W Turn to page 20 and find the word 'toxic'. Ask the children to define the word, and encourage them to look for clues to its meaning in the text.

C *(Clarifying)* Turn to page 30. Ask: *What is the story that Mrs Honey says is the best?*

Group and independent reading activities

Objective   Know how to tackle unfamiliar words that are not completely decodable (5.3). Read and spell less common alternative graphemes including trigraphs (5.4).

W On page 3, ask the children to find the word 'coin'. Ask them to sound out the phonemes all through the word (c–oi–n).

● Ask them to find other 'oi' words in the book ('pointed' page 5, 'noises/noise' page 7, 'oil' page 10) and to record them in a list.

● Ask: *Can you think of any other words with 'oi' in them?*

Assessment   *(R, AF1)* Can the children find other words with the 'oi' sound?

Objective   Read high and medium frequency words (5.5).
You will need high frequency 'ow' words written on card and placed in a bag ('how', 'low', 'now', 'grow', 'slow', etc.); blu-tack; table with two columns one for each 'ow' sound, drawn on the board.

W Ask children to find 'showed' on page 3 and then 'down' on page 4. Prompt children to tell you the different sounds the letter pattern makes.

● Draw out 'ow' cards from the bag and with the children's help position in the correct column on the board.

● Try 'tomorrow' and 'towards'.

Assessment   *(R, AF1)* Do children know that the word 'tomorrow' has the same 'o' sound as 'show'?

Objective Explore how particular words are used, including words and expressions with similar meanings (7.5).

You will need one large word card for each of these words: 'little', 'big', 'many', 'some'.

W Ask children to think of any other words that are similar in meaning to 'little' (e.g. small, tiny, minute, a bit). Write their contributions on the board, mentioning and discussing the term 'synonym'.

● Ask for synonyms for 'big' (e.g. large, enormous, giant, huge); 'many' (e.g. lots, a number, plenty, all kinds) and 'some' (e.g. a number, a few, not many, a selection).

● Ask volunteers to make a sentence from one of the word cards.

● Choose a different child to use the same sentence replacing the word with a synonym from the board.

● Write a sentence about Green Island on the board using one of the four words from the word cards.

● Invite children to rewrite the sentence using a synonym of their choice.

Assessment *(R, AF1)* Can the children read the sentences they have written?

Objective Give some reasons why things happen (7.2).

C *(Summarising)* Ask: *Why did the children go and see Mrs Honey?* (because of the oil on the seagull).

● Continue to ask questions, emphasising how one event leads on to another, e.g. *Why did the children go to Green Island?* (they took the otter back). *Why was it fortunate they went when they did?* (they saw the men).

● Talk about how the quick progression of events makes for an exciting and interesting story.

Assessment *(R, AF2)* Can children recall the sequence of events?

Objective Use context to build their store of vocabulary when reading for meaning (7.4).

C *(Clarifying)* Look at the signs and labels on pages 2, 6 and 21 with the children.

● On page 2, ask: *What words might be on the side of these boxes?*

● Repeat for the other pages, e.g. *What might there be on a lost property board? What might be on drums of toxic waste?*

- Establish what the signs and labels say.

Assessment (R, AF1) Do children attempt to read the signs and labels?

Speaking, listening and drama activities

Objective Adopt appropriate roles in small or large groups (4.1).

You will need a soft animal toy.

- Give the toy animal to a volunteer child and ask them to take on the role of Mrs Honey.
- Invite the other children to ask 'Mrs Honey' questions using the openers 'what', 'why' and 'how'.
- They must attempt to draw out how and what Mrs Honey does and why she thinks it is important.

Writing activities

Objective Draw on knowledge and experience of texts in deciding and planning what and how to write (9.1). Write simple and compound sentences and begin to use subordination in relation to time and reason (11.1).

- Ask the children to write down one reason why they think this is an important book to read. They should use a dictionary to help them spell unfamiliar words.
- Encourage children to use whole sentences such as 'I think... because...'.
- Let them take turns to read their answers to the group.

Assessment (W, AF2) Did the children write a complete sentence?

(W, AF3) Did they all give a valid reason, such as care for the environment?

(W, AF8) Did they use correct spelling and punctuation?

Storm Castle

> **C** = Language comprehension **R, AF** = QCA reading assessment focus
>
> **W** = Word recognition **W, AF** = QCA writing assessment focus

Group or guided reading

Introducing the book

C *(Prediction)* Together look at the cover. Ask the children: *Do you think this might be a 'real life' story or a magic key adventure? Why do you think so?*

C *(Prediction, Clarifying)* Read the title and ask the children to try to guess where the characters might be trying to go. Look through the book to see if the children are right.

Strategy check

● Remind the children to read to the end of a sentence and then reread it if they are uncertain about it.

Independent reading

● Ask children to read the story. Praise and encourage them and if they get stuck, help them to think of ways they might work out what a word means.

W If children struggle with some unfamiliar or new words, e.g. 'favourite' page 3, remind them to split the word into syllables and sound out the phonemes all through the word (f–a–v–ou–r–i–te).

C *(Summarising)* Ask children to retell the story in no more than 10 sentences.

Assessment Check that children:

● *(R, AF1)* can read on sight high frequency words

● *(R, AF3)* use comprehension skills to work out what is happening in the story.

Returning to the text

C *(Summarising, Clarifying)* Ask: *Which problem did Kipper solve?* (the monster). *Which problem did Biff solve?* (the floor). *Which did Chip solve?* (the giant robot). *How did they each do it?*

C *(Clarifying)* On page 9, ask: *Why did Biff say, 'It's a good job Nadim is with us'?*

W On page 17, ask children to find two words that have different spellings of the phoneme 'ee' ('three' and 'key').

C *(Clarifying)* Turn to page 20. Ask: *Show me how you think Kipper said 'that's funny'. Show me a different way of saying it.*

Group and independent reading activities

Objective Draw together ideas and information from across a whole text, using simple signposts in the text (7.1).

C *(Clarifying)* Write the following questions on the board and read through them with the children:
What is the title of the book?
Who is the publisher?
When was the book first published?
What are the names of the other stories in the series?
Who do you think the author is? (Roderick Hunt)
Who do you think the illustrator is? (Alex Brychta)
Where and what is the 'blurb'?

● Find another book in the series and discuss which features of the book's cover are the same and which are different.

● Discuss why the design is important as it identifies the book as part of the Oxford Reading Tree series.

Assessment *(R, AF4)* Do the children understand the different functions of author, illustrator and publisher? *(R, AF2)* Can they differentiate between the information found on front and back covers of books and their purposes?

Objective Give some reasons why things happen or characters change (7.2).

C *(Summarising)* Ask the children to choose one character and follow that character's part in the story from the beginning to the end.

- Can they find a point in the story where their chosen character's opinion of something changes, e.g. Wilf, Chip and Biff are frightened of the monster but change their minds when they realise the monster is friendly.
- Does their chosen character do something that has an influence on events in the story, e.g. Wilf pushing the door open on page 17.

Assessment *(R, AF3)* Do children form a clearer picture of the role their character plays in the story's plot?

Objective Read high and medium frequency words independently and automatically (5.5).

- **W** Ask the children to look through the book and tell you any words they come across that are to do with buildings or structures.
- Write the words on the board: 'bridge', 'castle', 'door', 'doorway', 'floor', 'gate', 'hall', 'house', 'keyhole', 'map', 'maze', 'mirror', 'room', 'school', 'wall'.
- Ask the group to form a circle. Designate one person to start. The children clap in unison and on the fourth clap, each child, in turn, says a word from the board or another building word.

Assessment *(R, AF2)* Do the children find relevant words in the text?

Objective Read and spell less common alternative graphemes including trigraphs (6.2).

- **W** Tell the children they are going to find words with the phoneme 'ay'.
- Turn to pages 4 and 5 and ask them to tell you each word they find.
- With the help of the children, record the words on the board under the appropriate headings ('a-y', 'ea' and 'ay').

Assessment *(W, AF8)* Do the children recognise the different spelling patterns?

Objective Engage with books through exploring and enacting interpretations (8.2). Listen to others in class, ask relevant questions (2.1). Work effectively in groups (3.2).

- **C** *(Imagining)* In small groups, ask the children to plan another challenge that the characters have to overcome in the Storm Castle.
- Ask each group to explain their challenge to the rest of the class.

- Encourage children to ask the presenting group questions about their challenge.

Speaking, listening and drama activities

Objective Explain ideas... using imaginative and adventurous vocabulary (1.3). Listen to others in class, ask relevant questions (2.1).

- Ask the children to imagine Nadim's robot and then describe what they would look like as the robot to a partner. They can use ideas from the story but must add at least two original ideas to their 'picture'.
- Encourage the children to ask questions of the robot to obtain further details of its appearance.

Writing activities

Objective Maintain consistency in non-narrative, including purpose and tense (9.3).

- Explain that the children are going to prepare some instructions for anybody wanting to know how to progress through Storm Castle.
- Discuss the challenges that the characters had to overcome and how they did it.
- Prepare brief notes on the board, e.g.

key hole door	hall of squares
monster	robot
maze	

- Divide the group into five smaller groups and ask each group to write down the instructions for one of the challenges on a piece of paper. They can refer to the book for help.
- Gather all the instructions together and talk about how best to lay out the information, e.g. using bullet points, such as:
  Open the door shaped like a key hole.
  Don't be frightened of the monster, he will show you how to go through the maze, etc.
- Prepare an instruction list on A3 paper that can be displayed.

Assessment (W, AF2) Do children use imperative verbs?

Superdog

> **C** = Language comprehension **R, AF** = QCA reading assessment focus
>
> **W** = Word recognition **W, AF** = QCA writing assessment focus

Group or guided reading

Introducing the book

- Together, look at the cover. Ask the children: *Who is on the cover? What is hanging off his collar?*
- **C** *(Prediction)* Read the title and ask the children to guess why it is called 'Superdog'. Look through the book to see if they are right.
- **W** Point out unfamiliar words such as 'course' (page 6), 'hero' (page 14) and 'girder' (page 26) so that they will be familiar when the children come to read them.

Strategy check

- Remind the children to read to the end of a sentence and then reread it if they are uncertain about it.

Independent reading

- Ask children to read the story. Praise and encourage them while they read. Prompt where necessary and encourage them to use different strategies for working out new words.
- **C** Check their understanding and clarify any misunderstanding by asking a variety of questions that require recall, inference and deduction. For example, ask: *Why did the children make a course for Floppy? Why was there a story about Floppy in the newspaper?*

Assessment Check that children:

- *(R, AF1)* use a range of strategies to work out unfamiliar words
- *(R, AF3)* use comprehension skills to work out what is happening in the story.

Returning to the text

- **C** *(Questioning, Clarifying)* Ask: *Did the story remind you of another hero?*

Was Floppy as brave as Superman? What could Superman do that Floppy couldn't? Do you like stories about other superheroes?

C *(Questioning)* Explain to the children that this story is set in San Francisco, a city in the USA. Ask: *Why do you think the author decided to set this story in America?* (where most of the superhero films are set).

C *(Questioning)* Ask: *Which do you think was the bravest thing Floppy did?*

W Ask the children to look through the book and find as many different types of transport as they can and to write down the words. Are there any types of transport that are new to them? (tram, bus, pram, ship, car, helicopter).

Group and independent reading activities

Objective Spell with increasing accuracy and confidence, drawing on word recognition and knowledge of word structure, and spelling patterns (5.2).

W Turn to page 16. Ask the children to find a word with two syllables. Say the syllables.

- Make a list of the words suggested.

- Ask the children for help in spelling each syllable.

- Show the children where the syllable break comes by marking the break in the word.

- Ask: *Can you find any three-syllable words?* Record them.

Assessment *(R, AF1)* Do the children notice that some of the two-syllable words are made up of two separate words (handbag, Superdog)?

Objective Explain their reactions to texts, commenting on important aspects (8.1).

You will need copies of *Green Island*.

- Look at the characters and setting of each story.

- Discuss what makes the stories different from one another, e.g. different main characters, and what makes them the same, e.g. adventure stories where someone or something is saved.

C *(Summarising)* Thinking about the theme, characters and settings, ask each child to write three reasons why he/she likes or dislikes the story *Superdog*.

Assessment *(R, AF2)* Do the children refer to the text to support their opinions?

Objective Read high and medium frequency words independently and automatically (5.5).

You will need 'What', 'Where', 'When' and 'Who' word cards

W Ask the children some 'What', 'Where', 'When', 'Who' questions based on the story.

● Hold up the 'What' card.

● In pairs, the children take turns to ask each other questions about the text on pages 4 and 5 of the story using 'What'.

● Ask some children to tell the class their question.

● Repeat for the other words.

Assessment *(R, AF1)* Do the children know the words by sight?

Objective Read and spell less common graphemes including trigraphs (5.4). Write simple and compound sentences (11.1).

W Ask the children to scan the story to find as many 'ou' words as they can. In five columns (one for each phoneme sound), list some of their contributions on the board, making sure all the different sounds are included:
found, outside, round, shouted, trousers
couldn't, wouldn't
enough
thought, course
though

● Ask the children if they can think of any other similar-sounding words spelled with 'ou' and add them to the list (e.g. cloud, should, tough, bought, dough).

● Rehearse the words from the five lists together.

● Ask them to write a sentence containing three 'ou' words that all sound different, then invite some children to read out their sentences.

Assessment *(R, AF1)* Do the children read 'though' and 'thought' correctly?

Speaking, listening and drama activities

Objective Tell real or imagined stories using the conventions of familiar story language (1.2).

- In pairs, children take turns to be the boy who is saved by Floppy.
- Ask each child to explain to his/her partner what happened and how frightened they were.
- Encourage the pairs to ask questions of each other when in the role of the boy.
- When each child has had a turn, the pairs should check the accuracy of their accounts against the book.

Writing activities

Objective Sustain form in narrative (9.2).

- Ask: *What is a superhero?* Talk about superheroes from books or comics.
- Ask the children to imagine they are superheroes. What super powers might they have: x-ray vision, superhuman strength, ability to change shape, mind-read?
- Write the headings 'character', 'setting', and 'story' on the board.
- Ask the children to choose a superhero name and a special power for themselves and to draft, then write and illustrate, a story about how they used this power to save an animal or a person from disaster. They should be guided by the headings.
- Discuss whether they should use the first or third person for their superhero.
- Collect the stories and make them into a 'Superhero Anthology' book for the book corner.

Assessment *(W, AF6)* Do the children use first or third person consistently.

The Litter Queen

> **C** = Language comprehension   *R, AF* = QCA reading assessment focus
>
> **W** = Word recognition   *W, AF* = QCA writing assessment focus

Group or guided reading

Introducing the book

C *(Prediction)* Together, look at the cover. Ask the children: *Do you think the lady is good or bad? Why do you think Chip is looking sad?*

- Read the title and ask the children to try to guess what the story is about. Look through the book to see if they are right.

- Point out the word 'microlight' on page 7 and explain what it is.

Strategy check

- Remind children of the strategies they can use if they meet a new word, e.g. split up into syllables, sound out the phonemes.

Independent reading

- Ask children to read the story. Praise and encourage them, prompting where necessary to work out new and unfamiliar words independently.

C *(Clarifying)* Check their understanding of the text and clarify any misunderstanding by asking a variety of questions that require recall, inference and deduction. For example, *Why was it a perfect day for a picnic? Why did Chip think he was not going to enjoy the adventure? What did Chip think when he had spread litter over the park? Why didn't Chip want to drop litter from the microlight?*

Assessment Check that children:

- *(R, AF1)* use a range of strategies to read for meaning
- *(R, AF3)* use comprehension skills to work out what is happening in the story.

Returning to the text

W Turn to page 2. Ask children to look for words with 'oo' in the middle. Ask: *Do these words rhyme? Can you think of words to rhyme with 'good' and 'food'?*

W Turn to page 11 and find 'home'. Ask: *Can you find another word with 'ome' in it?* (something). *Does it sound like 'home'? Can you think of a word that rhymes with 'home' and a word that rhymes with 'some'?* (dome, come).

C *(Clarifying)* Ask: *What did the Litter Queen like to do? Was she a kind, pleasant character? Show us the part of the story that tells us.*

C *(Questioning, Clarifying)* On page 22 ask: *Was Chip right to say that he didn't want to spread litter over the countryside? Why did Chip do as she told him in the end? What else could he have done? What would you have done?*

C *(Clarifying)* On page 29, ask: *What was it that Chip said that made Dad think he was ill?*

Group and independent reading activities

Objective   Draw together ideas from across a whole text (7.1).

● **You will need** a piece of crumpled up paper or crisp packet (litter) for each pair of children and a whistle.

C *(Summarising)* In pairs, ask the children, in turn, to describe to each other what happened to Chip in the magic key adventure.

● Each time the whistle is blown the children pass the piece of litter to their partner who continues the story.

● The children then check their retelling against the text.

Assessment   *(R, AF2)* Do the children tell the story in the correct sequence, use their own words and recall relevant details?

Objective   Spell with increasing accuracy and confidence drawing on word recognition and knowledge of word structure (6.1). Use commas to separate items in a list (11.3).

● **You will need** 10 of the following objects on a tray with a cloth to cover them: a banana skin, an apple core, a newspaper, a boot, a key, a tin can, a pair of glasses, a bottle, a milk carton, a light bulb, a piece of bread, a potato, a sheet of paper, a crisp packet, an empty toilet roll.

W Model writing the list of objects on the board, sounding out the phonemes on new and unfamiliar words and splitting the words into syllables. Wipe the words off the board.

● Let the children look at the 10 items laid out on the tray for two minutes, then cover them up.

● Ask them to write down all the things they remember seeing, starting the sentence 'I saw on the tray...', and using commas to separate the items.

● If they need help remembering the items, they could look at pages 26 and 27 of the book.

Assessment (R, AF1) Are the children able to spell the items correctly? (W, AF3) Do the children understand why they need to use commas in lists?

Objective Use syntax and context to build their store of vocabulary when reading for meaning (7.4).

W Ask the children to look at page 19 and tell you the word that describes how Chip says 'Oh, I don't like this'. Repeat on page 21 for how the Litter Queen says 'Come on! Come on!'.

● Encourage the children to think of other words to describe how Chip is talking (sadly, miserably) and how the Litter Queen is talking (angrily, grumpily).

● Write the following adjectives on the board: 'happy', 'sad', 'careful', 'cross', 'slow', 'quick'. Talk about how you can change these by adding the suffix '-ly', and that this describes how something is done. Ask the children to tell you the adverb in each case: happily, sadly, carefully, crossly, slowly, quickly.

● Ask children to think of some adverbs to describe how the family ate their picnic on pages 2 and 3 (happily, greedily, cheerfully, merrily, joyfully). It may help them if they think of some adjectives first.

Assessment (W, AF8) Do the children realise that some words change their spelling, e.g. 'happily', 'funnily', when you add '-ly'?

Speaking, listening and drama activities

Objective Speak with clarity (1.1). Listen to others in class (2.1).

You will need a blindfold and some pieces of 'clean litter' (the items should be distinctive and easy to describe).

- One child in the group is blindfolded.
- Hold up a piece of 'litter' and invite a child to say one thing to describe it without saying what it is.
- The blindfolded child has to guess what it is and may ask questions that can only be answered 'yes' or 'no' by the other children.
- Give other children a chance to be blindfolded.

Writing activities

Objective Draw on knowledge and experience of texts in deciding and planning what and how to write (9.1). Maintain consistency in non-narrative, including purpose and tense (9.3).

- Ask the children, in pairs, to design and make a poster listing rules for keeping school tidy. They should use a heading, e.g. 'Keep our school spotless', and sub-headings, e.g. 'Classrooms', 'Hall', 'Playground'.
- Once the children have checked their writing for correct spelling and sense, the posters could be displayed around the school.

Assessment *(W, AF2)* Do the children use the style and conventions of instructional writing? *(W, AF7)* Do they choose appropriate vocabulary?

The Quest

> **C** = Language comprehension   **R, AF** = QCA reading assessment focus
>
> **W** = Word recognition   **W, AF** = QCA writing assessment focus

Group or guided reading

Introducing the book

C *(Prediction)* Together, look at the cover and the illustration. Ask the children: *Who do you think the little man is? Can you suggest what kind of story this might be?*

C *(Clarifying)* Ask the children to read the title and explain to them what a 'quest' is.

W Look through the book and together work out the tricky words 'gnome', 'crystal' and unfamiliar words like 'unicorn' and 'basilisk'.

Strategy check

● Remind children to read with intonation and expression appropriate to the grammar and punctuation.

Independent reading

● Ask children to read the story and to find out what was special about the bell, and how they persuaded Grimlock to give it back.

● Praise children for reading with expression and adopting a different voice when reading Wilma's story.

C *(Summarising)* When they have finished reading, ask the children to give a summary of the quest story in no more than five sentences.

Assessment Check that children:

● *(R, AF1)* recognise the words 'girl', 'her', and 'burned' all represent the vowel phoneme 'er'

● *(R, AF1)* use a range of strategies to read for meaning

● *(R, AF3)* use comprehension skills to work out what is happening in the story.

Returning to the text

C (Questioning) On page 10, ask: *Why did Grimlock think it would be better if he appeared to Wilma as an old woman?*

C (Clarifying) Say: *Describe the Land of Ulm at the start of the story, the middle and the end.* Ask: *Why didn't Grimlock care that all the beauty went out of Ulm when he took the bell?*

W Ask the children to find pages 11, 17 and 21. Say: *Find the questions beginning with the words 'What...', 'Why' and 'How'. What are the answers?*

C (Questioning) On page 27, ask: *Why didn't the sound of the bell hurt Wilma and the Gnome's ears?*

C (Questioning) Ask: *What was the bravest thing Wilma did in the quest?*

Group and independent reading activities

Objective Draw together ideas from across a whole text (7.1). Explain their reactions to text, commenting on important aspects (8.3).

● **You will need** a small ring; some stories that involve a wish, e.g. The Three Wishes, The Frog Prince, Cinderella, Beauty and the Beast, Sleeping Beauty, etc.

C (Summarising) Talk about the 'wish' stories that you have gathered together. Ask the children to sit in a circle. Invite one child to hold the ring and tell the group a brief summary of one of the stories or any other 'wish' story they know.

● Encourage other children to offer to tell other 'wish' stories, but they only do so when they are holding the ring.

● Talk about and discuss the different types of wish, e.g. stories/wishes granted by good characters, those stories granted by bad characters; how the stories begin and how they end; who the characters are, e.g. kings, queens, princesses or princes; animals; mythical creatures, etc.

● Ask the children to write a few sentences describing their favourite 'wish' story and why they like it.

Assessment (R, AF7) Do children recognize that the stories are traditional stories. (R, AF3) Do the children use comparative words such as 'prefer', 'better', 'more'?

Objective Read high and medium frequency words independently and automatically (5.5). Compose sentences using tense consistently (present and past) (11.2).

- **You will need** the following word cards: 'see', 'saw', 'go', 'went', 'is', 'was', 'take', 'took', 'begin', 'began', 'know', 'knew', 'make', 'made', 'come', 'came'.

- Ⓦ Put four cards in the four corners of the room. Choose a child to go into each corner. The children pick a card and make a sentence using that word correctly. Repeat until the cards have all been used up.

- Write 'present' and 'past' as headings on the board. Read the cards and together decide which heading they should go under.

- Children then attempt to write an account of what they did yesterday using four words from the 'Past' list.

Assessment *(R, AF4)* Do the children know that the past tense is used when writing about something that has already happened and the present tense is used when writing about something that is happening now?

Objective Spell with increasing accuracy and confidence (6.1). Read and spell less common alternative graphemes (6.2).

- Ⓦ Teach the children the following rhyme with appropriate actions:

Touch your ear
Touch your head
Now, dear
Touch your toes instead.

- Write 'ear' and 'dear' together, and 'head' and 'instead' together on the board.

- Say the rhyme a few more times accentuating the four key words.

- Ask for some more examples of words that sound similar.

- Explain that the 'ea' phoneme often has different sounds in different words.

- Tell the children they are going on a quest to find words with different 'ea' sounds in the storybook. Working in pairs they should write down the words in lists according to their similar sounds: meant, read, bear; years, hear, reached, dear, really, ears, leaves, tears, read; great, break.

- Ask them to underline the words that have the same sound as the 'ea' sound in the rhyme.

Assessment *(R, AF1)* Do the children understand that the word 'read' can be pronounced in two different ways?

Speaking, listening and drama activities

Objective Adopt appropriate roles in small or large groups (4.1).

You will need a picture of a bell or a real bell.

- Look at all the pictures that have Grimlock in them. Ask the children to freeze-frame statues of Grimlock, trying to convey his different characteristics.
- Talk about the different ways Wilma managed to foil Grimlock (riding away on the unicorn; defeating the dragon with the lemon; defeating the basilisk with the mirror; making her wish in the castle).
- Pass the bell around the group. When a child holds the bell, he/she pretends to be Grimlock and tells the other children one of the ways in which he was 'foiled' by Wilma. Remind the children that they should sound very fed up and annoyed.

Writing activities

Objective Draw on knowledge and experience of texts in deciding and planning what and how to write (9.1). Use planning to establish clear sections for writing (10.1).

- Show the children how to write a plan for Wilma's story: title, opening words, main characters, settings, the problem, the solution.
- Ask the children to help you fill in each section.
- Encourage them to write their own story plan for a different quest.
- Use an extended writing time to allow children to write their quest story.

Assessment *(W, AF1)* Were children able to identify the different elements in the story and make contributions? *(W, AF8)* Were they able to use imaginative vocabulary?

Survival Adventure

C = Language comprehension   *R, AF* = QCA reading assessment focus

W = Word recognition   *W, AF* = QCA writing assessment focus

Group or guided reading

Introducing the book

C *(Clarifying)* Together, look at the cover. Ask the children: *What are the children doing? Who is with them? Do you think this is a modern day story?*

C *(Prediction, Clarifying)* Read the title. Discuss what survival means. Ask the children to guess what the story is about. Look through the book at the pictures to see if they are right.

● Talk briefly about people travelling across America to find new homes just over 100 years ago.

Strategy check

● Remind children to read with intonation and expression appropriate to the grammar and punctuation.

Independent reading

● Ask the children to read the story. Praise and encourage them while they read.

C *(Questioning, Clarifying, Prediction)* Check their understanding and clarify any misunderstanding by asking a variety of questions that require recall, inference and deduction. For example, ask: *Do you think Biff's umbrella is going to be useful? Do you think Amy was right to go off on her own? Why was everyone pleased that Biff had brought her umbrella?*

C *(Clarifying)* Ask the children if Biff was really frightened at the end of the story. Why not?

Assessment Check that children:

● *(R, AF1)* have secured reading and spelling of high frequency words

- (R, AF1) use various strategies to work out unfamiliar words
- (R, AF3) use comprehension skills to work out what is happening in the story.

Returning to the text

C *(Clarifying)* Explain that the story is fiction, but that the setting is based on fact. Ask the children to look in the text and at the illustrations to find something that is based on a fact, e.g. the wagons were pulled by oxen; trappers set traps to catch animals, etc.

C *(Clarifying, Imagining)* On page 2 ask: *Why would each item in the boys' survival box be useful? Tell me what they used the items for in the story. What would you take?*

W Ask the children to find all the words in the book that are made up of two words, e.g. 'notebook'.

C *(Clarifying)* On page 8: ask, *What was it, do you think, that the bear didn't like about the umbrella?*

C *(Clarifying)* Talk about the setting for the story. Ask the group to find clues in the text to show that the story is set in another country.

W Ask the children to find the word 'her' on page 7. Ask one child to explain why 'his', 'my' or 'their' would not do instead.

Group and independent reading activities

Objective Explore how particular words are used, including words and expressions with similar meanings (7.5).

W Ask the children to look through the book and find all the instances where the author has used 'suddenly' (pages 5, 9, 17, 19, 20 and 24).

- Discuss what 'suddenly' means and how it indicates to the reader that something happened very quickly and without any warning.

- Talk about what other words could be used instead of 'suddenly' in each of the places found, e.g. 'without warning', 'all at once', 'before she knew it', 'quickly', 'as quick as a flash', 'the clouds opened', etc.

- In groups, ask the children to choose one of the instances of 'suddenly' in the story and rewrite the sentence using an alternative word or expression.

Assessment *(R, AF5)* Can children find any other words in the text that the author likes to use?

Objective Engage with books through exploring and enacting interpretations (8.2).

C *(Imagining)* Turn to page 24 and talk about Biff's reaction to the arrival of Little Fox's father.

- Ask: *What would you have done? Would you have been frightened?*
- In turn, ask the children to imagine they are Biff or one of the other children. Encourage them to tell you what they would have done and how they would have felt being startled by visitors in the dark.
- Ask: *What other dangers might the children have come across camping out in the wild?*

Assessment *(R, AF3)* Can the children empathise with the characters in the story?

Objective Spell with increasing accuracy and confidence (6.1). Read high and medium frequency words independently and automatically (5.5).

You will need to write the following words from the story on the board: 'again', 'could', 'down', 'house', 'laugh', 'little', 'people', 'some', 'where', 'who'.

W Go through the words with the children.

- Cover the words on the board.
- Give each pair of children a piece of paper and a pencil.
- In turn, one child from each pair comes up and hears you say each word in his/her ear, then returns to their partner who writes down the word.
- Continue until all 10 words have been written down.
- Reveal the words and ask the children to check their spellings.

Assessment *(W, AF8)* Do all the children attempt to spell all the words?

Speaking, listening and drama activities

Objective Explain ideas (1.3). Listen to others in class, ask relevant questions (2.1). Work effectively in groups by ensuring each group member takes a turn (3.1).

- Look at page 9 with the children and find what Amy says when she is caught in the trap. Say the words using plenty of expression.

- Discuss with the children what else Amy could have said, e.g. 'Can anyone help me, please?' 'Is there anybody there to help me?' 'Please can somebody come and help?'
- In a circle, children take turns to be Amy. Each child has to try to think of a new way to ask for help using plenty of expression.
- Repeat for when Little Fox asks the other children to be quiet on page 20.

Writing activities

Objective Draw on knowledge and experience of texts in deciding and planning what and how to write (9.1). Use planning to establish clear sections for writing (10.1).

- Ask the children: *Have you ever been lost or lost something that is precious to you? Talk about what and where it happened and how it felt.*
- On the board write a scaffold for a story called 'Lost!' starting 'Once upon a time...' at the top; 'Then...' in the middle; and 'At last...' towards the bottom.
- Each child should use the model to write their own story based on a real experience or a made up one.

Assessment *(W, AF1, AF3)* Do children identify the different stages in their story?

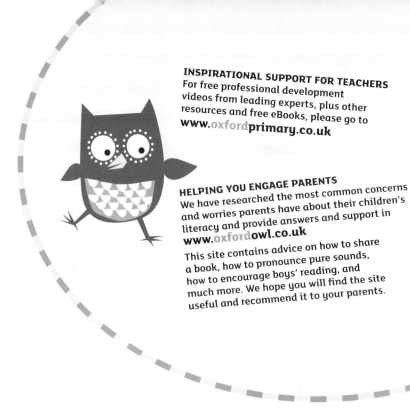

INSPIRATIONAL SUPPORT FOR TEACHERS
For free professional development
videos from leading experts, plus other
resources and free eBooks, please go to
www.oxford**primary.co.uk**

HELPING YOU ENGAGE PARENTS
We have researched the most common concerns
and worries parents have about their children's
literacy and provide answers and support in
www.oxford**owl.co.uk**
This site contains advice on how to share
a book, how to pronounce pure sounds,
how to encourage boys' reading, and
much more. We hope you will find the site
useful and recommend it to your parents.

OXFORD
UNIVERSITY PRESS

Great Clarendon Street, Oxford OX2 6DP

Oxford University Press is a department of the University of
Oxford. It furthers the University's objective of excellence in
research, scholarship, and education by publishing worldwide in

Oxford New York
Auckland Cape Town Dar es Salaam Hong Kong Karachi
Kuala Lumpur Madrid Melbourne Mexico City Nairobi
New Delhi Shanghai Taipei Toronto

With offices in

Argentina Austria Brazil Chile Czech Republic France
Greece Guatemala Hungary Italy Japan Poland
Portugal Singapore South Korea Switzerland
Thailand Turkey Ukraine Vietnam

Oxford is a registered trade mark of Oxford University Press
in the UK and in certain other countries

Text © Oxford University Press 2008

Written by Gill Howell, based on the orginal characters created
by Roderick Hunt and Alex Brychta.

The moral rights of the author have been asserted

Database right Oxford University Press (maker)

First published 2008
This edition published 2011

British Library Cataloguing in Publication Data

Data available

Cover illustrations Alex Brychta

ISBN 978-0-19-848357-1

10 9 8 7 6

Page make-up by Thomson Digital

Printed in China by Imago

Paper used in the production of this book is a natural, recyclable
product made from wood grown in sustainable forests. The
manufacturing process conforms to the environmental
regulations of the country of origin.